2009 Poetry Competition

I have a dream 2009

Words to change the world

Martin Luther King

John Lennon

Somerset

Edited by Mark Richardson & Lisa Adlam

First published in Great Britain in 2009 by:

 Young**Writers**

Young Writers
Remus House
Coltsfoot Drive
Peterborough
PE2 9JX
Telephone: 01733 890066
Website: www.youngwriters.co.uk

Foreword

'I Have a Dream 2009' is a series of poetry collections written by 11 to 18-year-olds from schools and colleges across the UK and overseas. Pupils were invited to send us their poems using the theme 'I Have a Dream'. Selected entries range from dreams they've experienced to childhood fantasies of stardom and wealth, through inspirational poems of their dreams for a better future and of people who have influenced and inspired their lives.

The series is a snapshot of who and what inspires, influences and enthuses young adults of today. It shows an insight into their hopes, dreams and aspirations of the future and displays how their dreams are an escape from the pressures of today's modern life. Young Writers are proud to present this anthology, which is truly inspired and sure to be an inspiration to all who read it.

Contents

Minehead Middle School

Ravenswood Special School

West Somerset Community College

The Poems

I Have A Dream

I have a dream,
That I will succeed in what I do,
I have a dream,
That I want to come true.
I have a dream,
That I will have friends forever,
I have a dream,
That we will stick together.
I have a dream,
That my lucky number is four,
I have a dream,
That I'll win the lotto and more.
I have a dream,
That there'll be peace on Earth,
I have a dream,
That people will see what I'm worth.
I have a dream,
That I'll be loved and sweet,
I have a dream,
That my life will be complete.
I have dreams,
Just like you,
I have dreams,
That I want to come true.

Abigail Pitchforth (12)
Bruton School for Girls

I Have A Dream

The world is good but also bad
Some things that happen make me sad.
I dream that people don't care
What colour, religion or what you wear!

I dream the troops never have to fight
Instead they sleep in safety at night.
I dream that people get along
And people know right from wrong.

I dream that there is no credit crunch
And people don't fight or punch.
I dream that I can control the weather
And that people work more together.

Charlotte Hunt (12)
Bruton School for Girls

I Have A Dream!

I have a dream,
To fly up high,
Float in the air,
Up in the sky.

I have a dream,
To see the world,
To see all the villages,
Every boy, every girl.

I have a dream,
To search outer space,
To see the stars,
In every place.

I have a dream,
To search down low,
To watch the seas,
And the mermaid shows.

I have a dream,
I'll rule the land,
The space and the sky,
The sea and the sand.

I have a dream,
I have a dream
To see every place,
That can be seen.

Katie Hayman (11)
Bruton School for Girls

3

I Have A Strange Dream

I have a strange dream,
About many things,
My special story,
That I must sing:

I have a strange dream,
That very soon,
Everyone will move,
To live on the moon.

I have a strange dream,
But not very big,
A monkey will dance,
While wearing a wig.

I have a strange dream,
That soon there will be,
A bee so small,
You just can't see.

I have a strange dream,
That soon one day,
Someone will invent,
Self-stacking hay.

I have a strange dream,
But not for long,
A cow will stand up,
To sing his song.

I have a strange dream,
Some weird, some fun,
My special story,
That I've now sung!

Rebecca Cole (12)
Bruton School for Girls

I Have A Dream

I have a dream
That I stay with my friends
I have a dream
That we go through all the trends.

I have a dream
That we smile, we laugh
I have a dream
That we share things half and half.

I have a dream
That we all live together
I have a dream
That we stay friends forever.

These are my dreams
I want them to come true
These are all my dreams
And I will see them through.

Imogen Thornhill (11)
Bruton School for Girls

I Have A Dream . . .

One day I will travel the world,
Being all that I could possibly be.
I would love to be recognised;
For being me!

One day when I travel the world,
I want to see love not hate
Friendship not enemies
True love, not fate!

One day I shall travel the world
To set the people free.
I will go out looking
For the real me!

Katherine Hoskins (13)
Bruton School for Girls

I Have A Dream!

I have a dream
It's rather strange -
I want to live through one ice age.
I want to see
A woolly mammoth looking at me.
I want to hear
A caveman running away with fear.

I have a dream -
It's to turn the world green
For pollution is the meanest fiend.
I want to see
Endangered species live and breathe.
I want to hear
My child playing in the pure clean air.

Jemina Gibson Wyer (14)
Bruton School for Girls

I Have A Dream

I have a dream to never grow up,
But so far I've been out of luck,
My parents keep saying my teddies will be sold,
But I'm holding onto the feeling that I'll never grow old.

I look around to see my sister growing up fast,
And inside I know my childhood won't last,
I like to go on outings with my mum and dad,
But when I'm older I might be lonely and sad.

The fun and games will have to pass,
And I won't be colouring in every class,
The thought of that breaks my heart,
And I know my adult life is soon to start.

I want to fly with Peter Pan,
And dance underneath the sea,
I want to do what children can,
To receive the enchanted key.

Harriet Smith (13)
Bruton School for Girls

8

I Have A Dream

I have a dream of shopping in Spain,
I have a dream of eating in England,
I have a dream of ice skating in Iceland,
I have a dream of riding in Russia.
I have a dream that I will pack my cases,
To go and visit all these places.

I have a dream of skiing in Switzerland,
I have a dream of hopping in Hawaii,
I have a dream of surfing in Scotland,
I have a dream of gliding in Germany.
I have a dream that one day,
I can do this and not have to pay!

I have a dream of diving in Denmark,
I have a dream of flying in Finland,
I have a dream of cycling in Canada,
I have a dream of canoeing in the Canaries.
I have a dream that I dreamt last night,
A dream of me travelling to reach the light.

Zoe Spencer (14)
Bruton School for Girls

I Have A Dream

I hate it here
I must get out.
To a quiet place
With no bombs about.

The sirens go off
Everyone's scared.
I'm tired and confused
But nobody cares.

I dream of that place
That people call home.
That far distant place
That I've never known.

I have a dream
To run away.
To find a place
Where it's safe to stay.

Rebecca Rundle (13)
Bruton School for Girls

I Have A Dream

I have a dream that one day we will stop violence.
Everyone will unite and get on.
There will be no wars.
This is my dream.

I have a dream that we can stop damaging our world.
Everyone will be greener.
We will reduce, reuse and recycle.
This is my dream.

I have a dream that we can all have food
No one will live in hunger.
We will all have clean water.
This is my dream.

I have a dream that we will stop being cruel.
We will protect wildlife.
We won't kill them for their fur.
This is my dream.

If we did all this our world would be great.
We would live peacefully.
Everyone would be happy.
These are my dreams today.

Olivia Clayton (13)
Bruton School for Girls

Design A New Me

I'm a fashion designer, I'm a hairdresser,
With them both, maybe I can design a new me.
I'm a dancer, I'm a model,
With them both, maybe I can design a new me.
I'm a sister, I'm a mother,
With them both, maybe I can design a new me.
I'm your friend, I'm your enemy,
With them both, maybe I can design a new me.
I dream of many things I hope to be,
And dream of peace in every country.
One day people might ask me, can you please
Design a new me?
But I know I don't need to
Design a new me.
I just need to be me.

Danielle Myers (12)
King Alfred's School

Inspire And Dreams

Inspiring my dreams of working with animals
Imagining the animals' lives in cruelty.
A dream that will hopefully come true
Inspirations and dreams are real
Animals live in cruelty
Their lives are shattered, but hopefully not for long
A dream that hopefully will come true and alive
Dreams
Inspiration
And all real.

Alex Strein (12)
King Alfred's School

Dreams

I have one single dream,
And my heart is set in stone.
To this one thing alone,
My life would be complete.
If I became a doctor,
Helping all those people.
Saving all those lives,
Making people happy.
Sometimes it is sad,
But mostly very happy.
I'd love to help many
People live,
And not so many die.
That is all I dream.

Tallulah Harris (11)
King Alfred's School

Imagine

Imagine
Being special
Imagine
Being everything
Imagine
Having a colourful sports car
Imagine
Being sweet
Imagine
Meeting old friends.
Imagine all of that.

Jessica Lavis (11)
King Alfred's School

Imagine

Imagine
Being a make-up artist
Imagine
Being special
Imagine
Having a sports car
Imagine
Having dogs
Imagine
Meeting my old friends
Imagine that.

Sophie Dahms (11)
King Alfred's School

I Have A Dream

I have a dream
That all the guns have gone.
I have a dream
That all the knives have gone.
I have a dream
That all the wars will stop.
I have a dream
That the world is at peace.
I have a dream
Don't you?

Jake Chambers (12)
King Alfred's School

I Have A Dream - Rich Or Poor

Imagine
Nothing
Imagine
Everything
Imagine being in-between the two.
Or everything revolving around you.
Rich or poor, just try and ignore.
Why should we imagine
When we can have it all?
Rich isn't always the hitch
Because the poor we always ignore
Believe it and achieve it.

Kerrie Driver (14)
King Alfred's School

18

Imagine

Imagine each race was in peace amongst each other
Imagine poverty didn't exist
Imagine everyone was everyone's brother
Imagine that this happened.

Imagine there was no crime
Imagine everyone was equal
Imagine there was no racism
Imagine that this happened.

Imagine the world was a clean environment
Imagine that this happened.

Adam Boardman (12)
King Alfred's School

I Have A Dream

I have a dream
To be inspired, to inspire
Imagine a world with new things to be discovered.
To help the less fortunate
To be grateful for my fortunate life,
To have a roof over my head and food on my plate.
I wish for peace between each other, no crime, no war,
Health in our homes
And our community with equal life,
Where poverty doesn't exist, fair life
Where you don't need the sun, the moon or the stars to shine
To be happy and have a good time
No misery, no sad faces to see.

Shannon Edwards (13)
King Alfred's School

My Inspiration

You are my inspiration
I want to be like you
To pull on an England jersey
And score at Twickenham too.
You're not always the best player
But you always try your best
Because you're brave, kind and courageous
And you stand up to every test.
That's why you're my inspiration
And I think you're the best.

Matthew Dickinson (12)
King Alfred's School

I Have A Dream

I have a dream to be a footballer,
Play at Wembley in the cup final,
Play in a league home and away,
Have training every day.

I have a dream to be the best,
So much better than all the rest.

Imagine being a champion,
Imagine seeing all the fans cheering,
Imagine lifting the trophy.

I have a dream to be a footballer.

Neil A'Barrow (13) & Jonny Hunt (12)
King Alfred's School

Inspire, Inspire

Inspire, inspire the world around
Inspire, inspire in jobs and at work
Inspire, inspire me and my friends
Inspire, inspire and do not offend
Inspire, inspire all through the night
Inspire, inspire to do what is right
Inspire, inspire to try our best
Inspire, inspire to do the rest
Although you only live in my dreams
You inspire me to never be mean.

Christopher Clarkson (13)
King Alfred's School

I Think

When I look at the sky, I begin to think.
I think of my dream to become an actress.
I think of my surroundings, of what's going on around me.
I think of the bad things, the racism, the guns, the knives, the crime.
And I think of my friends, my family, myself.

A world of happiness, that's what I want.
If the world could stop and start again, could happiness appear?
I wish it could, for everyone's sake, happiness please appear.

So that is what I think of, that is what I dream.
If only it could happen, if only it would.
Happiness is important, always try to maintain it.
Life is short, so head for the best and enjoy it.

Emma Huddy (11)
King Alfred's School

A Short Word - Haiku

A dream needs to live,
You can make it come alive,
A dream can come true.

Harriet Dickinson (12)
King Alfred's School

I Have A Dream

I have a dream the guns stop
The trenches undug, people's lives saved not lost.
Seeing, not hoping their family and friends
Will come back alive from the living hell of war.

I have a dream, cruelty stops to the living
And dead animals, humans and nature.

I have a dream people are free of slavery
No people kept as prisoners and being abused
For just being themselves.

I have a dream the world is healed
But nobody can say my dreams will come true.

Rebecca Summers (13)
King Alfred's School

26

I Have A Dream

I have a dream,
I look back at it,
It is hard to look back at it,
I'm not too sure why,
I begin to search my head,
I come across a story,
It's about a man unicycling,
I become inspired,
And crave to have a go,
But I try and try and fall and fall.
Game over.

David Sims (14)
King Alfred's School

I Have A Dream

I have a dream that most people will have peace
I have a dream that I will be like my dad and have the same job
I will exceed my dreams if we all work together
I will exceed my dreams if I work hard and have enthusiasm
I will help my dreams exceed if I do my part and don't argue
I will help my dreams exceed if I get my GCSEs
I want to make my dreams happen so that people won't have wars
I want to make my dreams happen so that I have a luxury life
I will make my dreams happen
But only if I try because
'It's better to try and fail than to have never tried at all'.

Ryan Kew (14)
King Alfred's School

My Dream

I have a dream that I would be a professional footballer for Man United
I'm standing in Old Trafford
People screaming my name
'Curtis! Curtis! Curtis!'
I step up to take the deciding penalty in the final
My heart beats faster and faster
I strike the ball into my favourite stand
The screams of 'Goal' fill the stadium.
I fall to the ground in amazement
The game was won and the Champions League was United's.
It makes me feel great.
Come on United.

Curtis Sanders (13)
King Alfred's School

My Inspiration

I have a dream that I can fly into happiness
And from all my troubles that seem to have no end
Something that inspires me is all my friends
If they weren't there I would be alone
And have no one to share my secrets and fears with.

When I listen to your guardian angel I think of my life
And all the things I love, my friends and my family.
They are all there for me, for whatever I do.

In the future I want to belong, somewhere I won't be judged
For what I look like, just for who I am.
I also want a place where people can be happy,
Without war or destruction.
Just peace for everyone.
That's my inspiration.

Loren Wells (14)
King Alfred's School

Culture Dreams

I have a dream . . .
That you can believe in your culture, and no one cares.
Something that inspires me is . . .
The news because they say that people have been hit
And beaten for believing in their cultures.
When I look at this I wish it would all *stop!*
In future I want to see . . .
Everyone believe in their own cultures
And people don't pick on them.

Sophia Hurley (13)
King Alfred's School

Imagine

I have a dream of being an engineer
Something that inspires me is motor racing
I get inspired by Jamie Green and Darren Turner.

I have a dream of being an electrician
Helping put up lights and alarms
I get inspired by watching somebody else.

I have a dream of being a historian
I enjoy learning about WWI and WWII
History lessons inspire me.

I have a dream of being a landscape gardener
I enjoy cutting the grass and weeding
I get inspired by watching gardening shows.

I still don't know which dream I'll do
I'm still thinking about these things
Or maybe I'll do something completely different.

Ian Tiley (12)
King Alfred's School

I Have A Dream

Something that inspires me is photography.
When I look at a camera I just want to take photos.
In the future I want to be a million things.
Dreams are meant to be sweet.
Rough dreams are not true.
Everyone should have sweet dreams not rough.
Anyone can have dreams.
Many dreams come true.

Emily Crosby (12)
King Alfred's School

I Have A Dream

I have a dream
Or so it seems
It's only in my head.
No more hunger, war or suffering
It's all happiness from here,
I have a dream
I wish to see
It turn into reality,
Everyone will all make friends
No bullying or tension,
I have a dream
I hope succeeds
I want to change the future.

Emily Shortland (12)
King Alfred's School

I Have A Dream

I have a dream and I see the future
It is bright and wonderful
Peaceful and calm
It is truly wonderful
I have a dream and I see the future
There is no suffering
There are no wars
It is truly wonderful
I have a dream and I see the future
There is happiness and laughter
And blacks and whites are equal
It is truly wonderful.

Kirrilyne East (13)
King Alfred's School

I Have A Dream

I have a dream that children will not live in fear,
I have a dream that people will not wonder when they will eat again.
I have a dream that people will not be judged by their skin,
I have a dream that people will be at one with the world
And gods will work as one.
I have a dream that children can be friends and last forever.
I have a dream that black and white will be seen together once more.
I have a dream that we will not use the world's resources for our
own enjoyment.
I have a dream that people will be at one with the world and gods will
work as one.

I have a dream and love and peace is my dream.

Charlotte Davey (13)
King Alfred's School

I Have A Dream

I have a dream that some day
I will be someone big
That I will be someone small
Turning big
I will conquer poverty
And make people proud.
I come from the small town
My inspiration has worked
It has pulled me through
Thanks to my inspiration
I have done my goal
My time for the
Community has been
Dealt.

Ellis Robinson (13)
King Alfred's School

I Have A Dream

I have a dream that wars and fights would end.
Then the world would be a better place for you and me.
The thing that inspires me is all those brave people fighting
Most people die and this is why I have this dream.
I would try and fix the world and make it a better place for you and me
All the people who fight for our country are my heroes.
In the future I could be someone who could change the world for
                                                    you and me.

I have a dream about the world being a better place.
I believe that I can make that happen
I hope others believe the same as me.

Kieran Rogers (12)
King Alfred's School

I Have A Dream

Imagine
If no one ever died
What would the world be?
Imagine
If everyone lived in the same building
Imagine
That you were famous
And that you had everything you wanted
Imagine
That every dream that you had came true
And that there were no rules
Imagine
If no one was there for you.

Bethany Criddle (13)
King Alfred's School

Dreams

D reaming of being a dancer
R otating and twirling my dance routine
E njoying the rhythm of dance
A nd falling into a dream
M oving gracefully my dream is my chance
S oon we'll be a dancing team.

Sasha Mills (13)
King Alfred's School

I Have A Dream!

I have a dream
That we all are united as one
I have a dream
No more suffering
I have a dream
No more poverty
I have a dream
No more guns
I have a dream
No more wars
I have a dream
No violence
I have a dream
We find a cure for cancer
I have a dream
We have no more criminals
I have a dream
That no one dies
I have a dream
And it is just a dream.

Adam Stringer (13)
King Alfred's School

Imagine

Imagine
A world with no hate
Imagine
Having a dream
Imagine
A pen in your hand
Imagine
A singer with no voice
Imagine
A ballet dancer with no music
Imagine
A CD but no player
Imagine
Scissors with no blades
Imagine
A frame with no picture
Imagine
A book with no pages
Imagine
A flower with no smell
Imagine
An ankle with no feet
Imagine
A bee with no sting.
Imagine
People with no dreams.
Imagine
A dog without a bite!

Colleen Tolfree (12)
King Alfred's School

I Have A Dream

I have a dream
About my grandad
Something that inspires me
Is my grandad's stories
He told me them when I was eleven
He makes them funny every time.
When I hear his stories he makes me feel happy.
When I am sad he tickles me
When I am older I want to be just like him.

Jason Saunders (12)
King Alfred's School

In The Future I Have A Dream

I dream that the rich help the poor
That's what I am going to do when I am rich
I will help
I will give
I will donate
My dreams will not be complete if I ignore this
I will help every colour, race and religion
I will give money, help and love
I will donate as much as I can
These are my rules to success and I will never forget them.

Callum Yates (11)
King Alfred's School

I Have A Dream . . .

I have a dream to work with the abandoned children who live on the streets or to work with the homeless.
I would nurse and tend to their wounds.

I am inspired by my mum and how she runs my family.
She teaches me how to appreciate people.
Also how to draw calmly.

I look at also being a nurse in a children's hospital because when I think of the children who are on life support machines and on the edge of dying my emotions run wild with sadness.

So one day I dream that these wishes come true.

Emily Sims (11)
King Alfred's School

I Have A Dream

I have a dream . . .
That I am rich,
That I will live in a mansion,
That I will drive 14 cars.

I have a dream . . .
That wars will stop,
That no man will take another's life.
That there will be world peace.

I have a dream . . .
That famine and drought will stop,
That racism will stop,
That crimes will stop.

I have a dream
I have a dream
I have a dream.

Ryan Cox (12)
King Alfred's School

I Have A Dream

When I look into the future I wish to see myself as a vet.
I have a dream to help animals of the world in any circumstances.
Something that inspires me is my pet dog
Who's always getting into a muddle.
When I look at animals in distress my emotions go out of control.
The person that inspires me is my dog's vet,
I'm not sure of his name but the work he does is amazing to me.
He knows about the medicines and treatment all the animals need,
This is the information I want to know when I am older.
This is my dream, it has been all my life.
These are my goals and the things that inspire me to do
What I want to do.

Alice-May Gates (12)
King Alfred's School

My Friend Poem

I have a dream that my friends are never horrible to each other and they
stop arguing and just be friends.
The person that inspires me is my friend Annabel.
When I look at Annabel I can always see a happy and smiley face.
If she is sad she won't take it out on anyone!
In the future I want me and her to be friends forever.

Holly Towler (12)
King Alfred's School

I Have A Dream

I have a dream that there's peace in the world.
I have a dream no one's poor.
I have a dream there's no wars.

Ashley Pincombe (12)
King Alfred's School

I Have A Dream!

I have a dream about having a happy life.
I have a dream about having children
And giving them a great life to live.
I have a dream about standing on mountains and to be free.
I have a dream about the sea flowing and the sand blowing.
I have a dream about having a smile on my face.
I have a dream about me having a great big white wedding
And bridesmaids with pink dresses.
I have a dream about having lots of money and giving my children
Anything that they want and having a big house
And a swimming pool in the garden.
I have a dream about having laughter in the air
And lots and lots of smiles.

Jade Merchant (12)
King Alfred's School

Imagine . . .

Imagine . . .
Black and white people can be as one.
Imagine . . .
Meeting all the people who have done things that have affected you.
Imagine . . .
Meeting your parents for the last time.
Imagine . . .
People not judging famous people by looking at them.
Imagine . . .
No more war, just peace all over the world.
Imagine . . .
If you could wish for anything, what would you do?

Chelsea Finch (12)
King Alfred's School

I Have A Dream

I have a dream that there will be no more war and fighting.
I have a dream no more people in this world will die in war.
I have a dream that all countries can live and work together
For a better world.
I have a dream no children will have to worry about their dads going to war.

I have a dream.

Luke Perrin (12)
King Alfred's School

I Have A Dream

I have a dream that my friends
Are never horrible to each other,
And we would never argue
And we would always get along.

Someone that inspires me is Holly
Because she is always good company
And really funny, I wish we
Would always be best friends.

Imagine that everyone would be
Friends and people would never
Argue and everyone got along
Really well.

Imagine a place where everyone
Was different and all got along
And respected each other and
Always helped each other.

Annabel Criddle (11)
King Alfred's School

I Have A Dream

I have a dream about being a footballer
The thing that inspires me is my mum
Because she lived on her own for a long time
She took me to football and she even helped train me in the garden
When I look at other people playing football I see them doing some
amazing things
When I'm older I would love to play for a football team.
If I had a chance I would.
If there is anything I could change I would be more confident.

Luke Jackson (11)
King Alfred's School

I Have A Dream

I have a dream
Where I want to be so much more than little old me.
I have a dream of being an actress or a singer if I can
I think of this in my mind's eye when silence is around.
But when life gets tough and the road is long,
It seems there is no light.
When the dreams you had somehow seem lost,
Don't ever give up or stop the fight.
If I do well at school and study really hard,
I'll go to drama school and find my shining light
I'll hold my head high and imagine all things possible,
If you only have a dream.
But until that day comes,
Looks like I will just have to keep on dreaming
And practising in the mirror,
With my hairbrush, singing.

Chelsea Court (12)
King Alfred's School

Imagine No World

Imagine no world for us to live
It's easy if you try
No animals or humans
Or myths and legends
Or food for us to try.

Imagine no countries for us to meet,
It's easy if you try
No religions or wild animals
Or Fairtrade products and
Love for us to try.

Imagine no England for our lives
It's easy if you try
No pubs or cinemas
Or the English breakfast
And no drunks for us to fine.

Imagine no city for us to live
It's easy if you try
No shops or theatres
Or lovely restaurants
And friends far and wide.

Matteo Palumbo (12)
King Alfred's School

I Have A Dream!

I have a dream,
That my mum can see out of two eyes.
Some people don't think enough!

I have a dream that,
My auntie can have her husband back,
And that she can get better.

I want to write a letter,
For things I want to change:
I want everything to be okay,
No violence, no wars!
When I am older, I want my
Mum to be proud of me.
I will try my hardest at everything.

I want to be a make-up artist when I'm older,
It really inspires me and art.

I want the world to be at peace,
No fall outs and more friendships.

Katherine Owen (12)
King Alfred's School

My Inspiration

People who travel the world inspire me.
They inspire me so much I want to be one.
I want to be a person who travels the world and sees places.
I want to jump on a plane and fly
And not return until I have visited everywhere.
I want to meet people from different countries
And take photos of the beautiful views.
See, my dream is to travel the world.
Some people say it's stupid to dream.
But I know that one day, as long as I keep believing in my dream,
It will come true.
One day I will get to travel the world
Because that's my dream.

Sarah Rees (12)
King Alfred's School

My Dad

My dad makes me want to be as good as I can!
Do school as good as I can!
Do work as good as I can!
Do 'as' good as I can!
My dad makes me be as good as I can be
Just like him!

Oliver Hancock (11)
King Alfred's School

I Have A Dream

To be the greatest millionaire ever
I could walk around with a suitcase and a feather
I would look so good all done up in leather
Throughout the day I will astray
Not knowing where to go
Honestly I will never feel low
I will have my own aeroplane
So I could fly all the way to Spain
With nice dunnys
Hot and sunny
Also I heard about some strange looking bunnies
When I return, fireworks will fly
Not too close to where I am in the sky
It will be difficult not to cry
I will return home
Get comfy in my dome
I will go out for a drink
Across the crumbly road
Of course avoiding all the toads
Setting my walking stick to a different mode
When my wife drives me round the bend
My life will
Finally
Come to an end.
The end.

Aaron Bird (11)
King Alfred's School

I Have A Dream

I have a dream for a world of good,
I have a dream for no bad just good,
I have a dream for you and me,
So we can live in perfect harmony
No wars, no fights,
No arguments anymore.

I wish for a world of good,
I wish all we heard of was good,
I wish for a world of love,
No hatred, only love,
Just one big brotherhood.

I hope everyone will dream,
A dream that could come true,
A dream just like mine,
So please dream along too,
This way our dream, one day may just . . .
Come true!

Rebecca Duckering (11)
King Alfred's School

I Have A Dream

I have a dream; the war in Afghanistan will end.
It's starting to drive me round the bend.
Too many people are dying and losing limbs,
I suspect they are feeling dim.
I wish the Taliban would give up,
Then the lads and girls from Britain can come home.
The family can see their daughter or son,
Then the war will be done.

Christopher Jones (13)
King Alfred's School

Untitled

I have a dream,
A dream that the war in Iraq will stop,
The US marines will find Osama Bin Laden,
The war on terror will stop,
No more hatred
When Bin Laden's dead.

Dominic Phillips (12)
King Alfred's School

Afghanistan War

The war drags on,
Two sides fighting for principles,
The army is doing right, trying to protect the people,
The Taliban are putting up a good fight,
The brave soldiers fight every day,
The country sees another dead soldier,
They sit and watch in dismay,
But for fighting in Afghanistan, it's just another day,
I have a dream,
A dream that the war will stop,
I hope one day, the fight in Afghanistan can be given the chop.

Ben Alderton (13)
King Alfred's School

I Have A Dream

I wish one day no one will suffer
And kids won't have to worry,
Whether their mum will be there in the morning.
While doctors hurry to make them better,
Why can't cancer go away?
At least for just one day!
It kills so many people
And hurts so many souls.
I have a dream it will all go away
At least for just one day!
I see people making jokes
How can they be so cruel?
When people die it's not right
All through the day and all through the night
Doctors, doctors try your best
To get rid of this awful mess!
Why can't cancer go away?
At least for just one day!

Aimee Collman (12)
King Alfred's School

I Have A Dream

(In loving memory of Julie Catherine Amy Wash who died on the 3rd March 2009)

I have a dream
That the crash never happened
That you are still with me

I still remember your grey curly hair
And the way you said things were fun

I still remember the last day I spent with you
The barbecue blazed and Michael yapped
We had a blast

Then off to Spain
In the aeroplane
You went without a doubt

I still remember
The day I found out
It was the 4th of March
That the day before you had died in a car crash

I have a dream
That the crash never happened
And you are still with me.

Rhiannon James (12)
King Alfred's School

Peace Poem

Oh why, oh why
Can't we just be friends?
Love one another, not have to pretend
All to be equal
We too can share
No racism
People can't stop and stare
We didn't need guns
No killing for fun
Let kids run free
Let them see the sun
Make love not war
Let's respect the law
Oh why, oh why
Can't we just be friends?

Mike Green (13)
King Alfred's School

I Dream

I dream of my future
In a uniform of blue
Will I be a policeman
Or join the fire services crew?
I stare at nature
Amazing and green
I hope my friends are like me
And inspired to keep it clean.

Joshua Fowler (12)
King Alfred's School

I Had A Dream!

I dreamed
I stopped war
Or I bought peace
I flew to the moon
And bought back a balloon
I dreamed
I was a success
And I tried my best.

Lauren Arnold (11)
King Alfred's School

I Have A Dream . . .

I have a dream
To see all those people who are lost and dead
Just one more time.

I have a dream
To help people in these countries
Who can't help themselves.

I have a dream
To fill peoples' tummies
Who can't be filled.

I have a dream
To save peoples' lives
Who cannot be saved.

Danielle Manlow (12)
King Alfred's School

Lean On My Dream

I have a dream that everyone will be free of poverty
Lean on my dream.
When I grow up I want to be famous and travel the world and help
the poor.

Lean on my dream
The people who inspire me are the people I see every day
Lean on my dream
There is a difference between life and death. I want to stop death.
Lean on my dream
I dream of a world where everyone is equal.
Lean on my dream
I dream of a world where there is no terror threat, and every
country is equal.

Lean on my dream
I have a dream where every religion is respected.
Lean on my dream
I have a dream where every child's life will be fair.
Lean on my dream
I dream of a world where there is no poverty, no war and no gangs.
Lean on my dream!

Becky Jones (11)
King Alfred's School

The World Around Me

I have a dream for everyone to have the perfect life.
To walk around the streets not scared of guns and knives.
To live in complete simplicity day and night.
For everyone to be equal, black and white.
To benefit from God's creatures scattered all around.
And to cherish all the nature laid across the ground.
To treat everyone and everything with utmost respect.
And to live in harmony with no hate or neglect!
I have a dream that tomorrow's possibilities happen today!

Chloe State (12)
King Alfred's School

I Have A Dream

I have a dream that one day
I will become one of the greatest game designers
Something that inspires me is nature
When I look at my friends
I see joy and forget about
Things that make me feel down
In the future I don't want any
Wars and everyone to be equal.

Connor Baker (12)
King Alfred's School

I Have A Dream . . .

I have a dream . . .
For everyone to stop hurting each other
All those knives, guns and weapons
What is the point?

I have a dream . . .
To stop all wars
People only die . . .
What is the point?

In the future . . .
It should all stop
Then all we hear is
Bang, bang, pop.

Lauren Powell (11)
King Alfred's School

I Have A Dream!

I have a dream to become a vet, to save animals,
To travel the world, to help them, my life long ambition!
All different animals, birds, mammals, reptiles, amphibians,
I'll help them all, I'll cure them, treat them, make them better!
This dream is going to be my job when I grow up and become an adult
I do have many other dreams that I want to fulfil! My dream!

I have a dream for when I grow up for me to travel the world,
There are many different places I want to visit,
I want to see, the sights would be amazing!
So many countries, hot and cold, across the world I want to see!
My other dream!

There are many things I want to complete.
I want to achieve, my hopes, my dreams,
I will succeed in whatever I shall do!
I have a dream . . . my dream!

Charlotte Dursley (12)
King Alfred's School

A Dream To Succeed

I have a dream
To be a pro footballer
While I have David Beckham inspiring me I can't fail.
I have a dream, a dream to succeed.
And everyone to succeed with me.
When I watch David Beckham playing
I think to myself that will be me soon.
I have a dream
To live my life happily.
I have a dream
To entertain people with my skills
And make them happy while watching the game.
I want a bright future
Where I'm living the dream.
Living my dream.

Morgan Sealey (12)
King Alfred's School

I Have A Dream

I have a dream to be a pilot.
N ot a fighter pilot but an airline pilot
S pain, France, Greece, Australia and America, I will fly to
P ilot R Howard sounds good to me
I n case of emergency I will land us safely
R adio in when help is required
A ltitude should be high so I don't crash
T ake-off and landing are the hardest part I hear
I n the air above the clouds I will soar
O n the ground I will run the checks
N ationwide I will fly . . .

Rob Howard (13)
King Alfred's School

I Have A Dream

I have a dream that this could be a better place,
I hope that will put a smile on everyone's face.
I have a dream that children stop getting abused,
I hope that more parents get accused.

I have a dream that this is a crime-free place,
I hope police are always on the case.
I have a dream that everybody is nice,
This is my dream!

Amy Harris (12)
King Alfred's School

No More School

I have a dream
If a world without school,
No English, no maths, art or science,
No drama, music support or RE
No more homework,
No more teachers
No more horrible school dinners.

Howard Manaton (12)
King Alfred's School

My Dream

I have a dream to become a PE teacher
Because I love sport and I would love to teach it too
Something that inspires me is my dad because
He likes his sport and he has inspired me to do a lot
Of sports like football and hockey.
When I look at my parents I think I would want to be like them
Because they have been and are successful.
In the future I hope I do become a PE teacher
And achieve all my dreams because that would be great.

Chelsea Fisher (12)
King Alfred's School

The Bike Mechanic

I want to own my own business,
I want it to run smoothly,
I want to earn lots of money,
I want to be a bike mechanic,
I want to fix bikes,
I want them to be safe for people to ride.
I want to employ people too.
Bikes are environmentally-friendly
Good exercise
Go pretty quick
And are fun too.

Jordan Bowcott (11)
King Alfred's School

I Have A Dream

I have a dream to become a footballer
Something that inspires me is football
I hope there is no school and no teachers
I want to play for Chelsea and earn a lot of money
I want to perform well with a lot of skill and score a few goals.

Ben Rispoli (11)
King Alfred's School

Dream

I had a dream
When I was little, I knew I was headed towards a great future.
A future I couldn't even imagine of having,
I had a dream.
That I would be a rock guitarist,
On tour 300 days a year
I had a dream that I would be an artist,
Selling paintings for millions
I had a dream
That I would be an actress
Acting in Hollywood movies
Instead, I'm sipping tea, sealing envelopes,
It was all a dream.

Ysabella Fernandez (12)
King Alfred's School

I Have A Dream

I have a dream that the world is like High School Musical
And that when I am older I am one of the characters of High School Musical.
Also I wish that I could sing and dance like them.

I want to be popular and to have loads of friends,
Write loads of songs like Kelsey in High School Musical
Because then with songs everyone will be happy.

I have a dream that I will be good at acting in a High School Musical movie.
I would like to create a new character to be in charge of the cheerleaders to
support the basketball team.

I want to make everyone part of High School Musical
To make the world happy with singing and dancing because it is so
much fun.

Eve Meehan (11)
King Alfred's School

I Have A Dream

I have a dream to be funny
And that dream is to be like Lisa Simpson
In that dream it is going
To be good, funny and interesting
That dream is a cartoon dream
That dream is a good dream.

I have an image in my head of what
I will be like when I do my ambition
Creating cartoons that will make people laugh
And jump out of their seats.

Josie Davis (11)
King Alfred's School

I Have A Dream

I have a dream,
That promises are kept and lies not told.
I have a dream,
That people do not get hurt and have no need for tears.
I have a dream,
That hearts cannot be broken, just filled.
I have a dream,
That people will not betray you or go behind your back.
I have a dream,
That my family will be okay again.
I have a dream
That good will come from this.
If only, if only dreams could come true,
But it's just a dream . . .

Harriet Lamb (13)
King Alfred's School

I Have A Dream

I have a dream
Almost every night
Of fear and love
Romance and fright.

I dream of
My parents meeting,
The first time they ever kissed,
Their wedding and the years that follow
All in a peaceful bliss.

But love may not last forever,
As cracks begin to show,
And now I will simply dream,
'Did they ever love each other so?'

Cora Burt (13)
King Alfred's School

I Have A Dream

I am inspired,
As a young teenage girl,
With an Olympic dream,
More valuable than a pearl.

The dream is very challenging,
Dedication is the key,
The key can be the star,
That will always follow me.

The star I'd like to follow,
It lights up the whole sky,
I want to follow in her footsteps,
Of which my dreams will fly.

I have a dream,
That my friends and family,
Will be proud of what I do,
As I want to be a swimming star like
Laura Manadou.

Kim Taylor (13)
King Alfred's School

I Have A Dream

A dream is something you believe in,
A dream is happiness when it comes true,
My dream is for people not to be so selfish,
To think about others who don't have the happiness we have,
For people to get animals from the RSPCA,
For families to eat everything on their plate,
For children to stop getting abused by their parents,
For peace to come and stop all terrorists,
For everyone's dreams to come true.

Ellen Sturdy (13)
King Alfred's School

I Have A Dream!

No beating of dogs or any animals.
Why do people do such things?
They're just so cute and helpless
What have they ever done to you?
They don't deserve to be beaten
I have a dream to change all this,
They need a loving home
You could give it to them
And also a great big bone.

Ellen Stevens (12)
King Alfred's School

I Have A Dream!

I have a dream
That Bristol City will go up a league.
That's a thing I really do plead
Really I hope I will always believe.
I hope that the Bristol City fans can be cider heads till they die
And they keep the red flag flying high.
I hope our new stadium goes as high as the sky
When we win we will jump so very high.
I hope we can beat Cardiff City
But to do that we must show no pity
We must chant as loud as we can
But people do swear including that old man.
But it's fun and the atmosphere's great
But these are some things that I really hate.
When the tall people in front of me stand up
And when the people drop their coffee cups.

Oliver Scott (13)
King Alfred's School

Dream

I have a dream . . .
And although it may seem,
That it's one of those dreams you have in your sleep.
In fact it's a dream to stop all kinds of cruelties,
A dream that one day I will be centre stage in the spotlight.
A dream that every problem and worry disappears,
A dream where I feel my toes in the sand and the sun beaming on my face.
A dream where I meet a celebrity full with inspiration,
If you believe, dreams really can come true.
If I can imagine them, can you?
Stop cruelty.

Gemma Robertson (12)
King Alfred's School

I Have A Dream

I had a dream . . .
That fighting was ended
And peace was attended
No murders of innocent people were committed
No war or rebelling was submitted.

There were never any fights
Because everyone was at peace
Children were safe enough
To be let off their leash.

But I sadly woke up, hearing a bang
I rushed out of my bed,
I looked out my window
To find another innocent man . . .
Shot dead.

Chloe Pugsley (13)
King Alfred's School

What Makes A Dream?

To have a dream,
Where everything is perfect, where nothing goes wrong
When a dream takes place, anything can happen,
You can be happy or sad, excited or distraught.
In a dream, anyone can be your friend,
Anyone can be there for you.
Anything can make a dream happen,
Your mates, a boyfriend, family or even a hobby
Dreams can sometimes confuse you
Or sometimes they reveal things.
That is what makes a dream.

Jodie Goss (13)
King Alfred's School

Inspiration

In the future
I want the world to be without war
I want to be an artist
Like Claes Oldenburg and Picasso
I want my art to be seen and appreciated
Claes Oldenburg inspires me by his
Super-sized art and Picasso inspires me
By his abstract art.

Andrew Francis (14)
King Alfred's School

Untitled

I have a dream to make lots of money
I want cool friends that are smiley and funny
I want to fish, I like to ski
I would love to do these professionally
Almunia is my idol
I want to be like him.

Stewart Kilmartin (13)
King Alfred's School

Bike Ride

I have a dream that one day I will be riding a motorbike
In the warm summer breeze.
Going quite fast but not being stupid,
Keeping an eye out for an idiot.
I wish that people wouldn't be silly
Just enjoy the ride in dignity.
I hate it when people ride with no sense
A T-shirt and trackies will not protect you.
But leathers and gloves and bike boots will
So don't be stupid, don't be silly
Ride with a little bit of decency.

Corey Hayes (14)
King Alfred's School

Badminton Is My Inspiration

Badminton is my inspiration
One-a-side
You might have to go wide
High or low?
What won't they know?
Will they return it
Or will they miss it?
Their serve
It might curve
Is it to the right
Or is it just my sight?
Badminton is my inspiration.

Steven Lyons (13)
King Alfred's School

A Ray Of Inspiration

When I look at Ben and Sam
All I see is a ray of inspiration
I feel I know more than Einstein
And I could write a book with Shakespeare

They inspire me, I'd be nothing without them
I believe people like them make the world
And all that is in it.

Jamie Hand (14)
King Alfred's School

I Have A Dream . . .

There will be no more violence in the world
And all the criminals will be hurled
There will be peace and harmony
Around the world for all to see

I know that there isn't now
But I think that somehow
There will be peace and harmony
Around the world for all to see.

Bradley Fisher (12)
King Alfred's School

Imagine

Imagine if the war stops,
The pollution would increase because no one would die in the war.
Imagine if people could come back to life
So you could see everyone in your family.
Imagine if everyone recycled
Then the world wouldn't be trashed or look so bad.
Imagine if you ask for anything and you get it
So you would pay for anything.
Imagine you could do whatever you want to do.
Imagine if nothing breaks
Then you wouldn't have to buy a new one.
Imagine if everyone showed everyone the same respect
As your family.
Imagine you couldn't die
Then you would see your family in the next 500 years.
Imagine you could see anything you want to see.

Jake Garrett (12)
King Alfred's School

I Have A Dream

Imagine, imagine a world with no school.
Play on my mini moto with my friend.
Play table tennis with my sister.
Play on my pool table every day.
Go over to the track on Tuesday and Thursday to practice.
Go over to the skate park to learn.
People come round to play in my mansion.
A school would be a better place.

Bradley Day (12)
King Alfred's School

I Have A Dream

I would love to be a star
My name up in lights
To have lots of cash and have a car that's flash
I'd love to be a singer
Up there with the stars
Just like Britney, Leona too
And also Lily Allen
That's the one, the one who inspires me.
So don't be down, have a dream
You never know, it might come true.

Scarlett Tagg (12)
King Alfred's School

I Have A Dream Job!

I have a dream job,
There's no need to sob
My life to be lived,
Might not be a fib.
Flashing my lights,
It's time to pull over.
I've caught you good,
Like I knew I would.
Policeman that must be it,
Yes my dream really fits.

John Sandilands (13)
King Alfred's School

I Am Sorry

I am sorry I ran away
I had nowhere to go
I had to go somewhere
But there was nowhere to go
Wherever I went you would follow
So I just ran away
I ran into the night
With only the streetlight for light
Then you found me
You were in so much distress
You were angry and sad all at once
But you were happy to see me
I ran away because I had nowhere to go
So please don't hurt me
I am sorry for running away
I am sorry.

Ed Sutton (12)
King Alfred's School

My Big Dream!

In my dream I was a . . .
Horse galloping through the gushing air,
And a tiger with an evil glare,
I was a bee with lots of honey,
And a handful of money.

I had a dream once I was a . . .
Bird singing at the top of the trees
And a robber nicking a set of keys
I was a raindrop falling down from the sky
And a monkey waving and saying goodbye.

My dream was to be a . . .
Fish swimming through the sea
And become a pirate with a crooked knee
That is my *big* dream!

Abi Connick (11)
King Alfred's School

I Have A Dream

I have a dream that I can fly
To the highest of high,
I have a dream that I could be
A professional footballer as good as David B,
I have a dream that I could be a bumblebee
As mighty as he.

I have a dream that I could see
Two dolphins diving in the sea,
I have a dream that I could dive
In the blue ocean far and wide,
I have a dream that I could play,
In the circus all day.

I have a dream that I could drive
The hottest car of my life,
I have a dream that I could heal
A million people on the battlefield,
I have a dream that I could eat
A great amount of chillies and meat.

Jacob Burt (12)
King Alfred's School

Love

I love you for so many reasons
Big and small and all of them are wonderful

I love you because of what you do for me
That's what makes you one of a kind . . .
The only one in the world for me . . .

I love you because of what you do for me and the
Special things we do together . . .
I love you
Just because I do

And, my heart belongs to you forever onwards,
'Cause I love you for who you are . . .

Liam McLauchlan (11)
King Alfred's School

My Future World

I see a world with no dark face
In my world lies kindness and grace.
There is no black, there is no white
For in my world all colours are right.

There is no fighting, there is no war,
And in my world there won't be, that's for sure.
There is no pollution or grey skies
And in my world there are no lies.

There is no hunger, there is no thirst
For in my world *all* people's needs come first
There are no killers, there's not one thief
And in my world there is no grief.

There is no rich, there is no poor
In my world there's no class system anymore
No one's called stupid, idiot or nerd
In my world *all* voices are heard.

If you want all of these things to come true,
Then my future world is the world for you.
You may think I'm crazy, you may think I'm mad,
But this is the dream I've always had.

Lucy Cox (12)
King Alfred's School

I Have A Dream Of Drumming

I have a dream of drumming
Not running.
I dream of music
Not a cue stick.
I dream of Glastonbury Festival
Not a particle.
I dream of fun
Not sun.
I dream of parties
Not pasties.
I dream of sub-woofer
Not a dog walker.
I have a dream of drumming.

Michael Welsh (11)
King Alfred's School

Untitled

As I walk the walk of a teenager,
I am always getting bored,
Too old to play childish games,
And write silly messages on a blackboard.
I look at people, older, and think what am I going to be?
The life of a model, teacher, or whatever,
It seems like hard work to me.
I guess that's the future then,
For now it's MSN.
We'll talk about our hobbies,
Make-up, music and the boys
It was always so much easier when I
Could play with all my toys.

Roxanne Fisher (14)
King Alfred's School

I Have A Dream!

I have a dream,
All wars will stop,
No need to kill,
No need for cops.

I have a dream,
World peace is here,
And everyone,
Can give a cheer.

I have a dream,
That no one dies,
We can stop,
All these cries.

I have a dream,
We'll all succeed,
We'll cater for,
Every need.

I have a dream,
All wars will stop,
No need to kill,
No need for cops.

Heather McCall (11)
King Alfred's School

My Inspiration

You are my inspiration
My inspiration is you
Without you I would be nothing
I wouldn't be here
You are the one who cares
You have been through a lot
But I know you are a fighter
I am a pain
But you put me straight
I can't believe I nearly lost you
That would be my heart gone
I wouldn't cope
Without you Mum
You are my life
My life is yours!

Amy Fitzpatrick (13)
King Alfred's School

I Have A Dream

I have a dream to make people aware
Of what they are doing to their planet.
I have a dream to help prevent cancer
And rid the illness altogether.
I have a dream to stop all kinds of animal testing.
I have a dream to stop all kinds of violence.
I have a dream to prove that all people should be equals.
I have a dream to be the best that I can be.

Daniel Sykes (13)
King Alfred's School

Inspiration

I have a dream to live on a sandy beach
N owhere else is more peaceful
S o when I sleep at night I can hear the almost silent sea dragging in
    and out
P ine trees surround me
I can run my fingers through the silky sand
R un through the salty warm water
A nd eat the delicious fruit from the trees
T he island is only populated by one person, me
I t would be incredible
O cean surrounds the island
N o one but me.

Stephen Leyshon (13)
King Alfred's School

A Small Little Squirrel

A small little object runs through the trees,
A small little squirrel maybe it could be,
A small little head,
A small little body.

I wish I could climb like it,
I wish I could climb to the top,
I wish I was small and nimble.

But I guess at the end,
At the end of the day,
For all of us there's just one problem,
We're only human.

Stephen Lilley (14)
King Alfred's School

I Have A Dream

Everyone should have a dream.
So dreams can come true.
Some people have too many.
But some only two.

You have to chase it well,
Anywhere it goes.
To make it really happen,
You just have to follow your nose.

A dream can be anything,
Anything you want it to be.
Always try and fulfil it,
You can do it just like me!

Charlotte Caulton (13)
King Alfred's School

I Have A Dream

I have a dream
That I will be successful in the future,
That I will be the best that I can be.

I have a dream
Something that inspires me is the army,
They risk their lives for us to have a future.

I have a dream
When I look at a great successful person
I know that they worked hard for it.

I have a dream
In the future I want to be like those successful people
I will be the best that I can be.

I have a dream!

Matthew Alderton (14)
King Alfred's School

I Have A Dream

I have a dream . . .
There will be world peace.
Conflict everywhere will stop!

I have a dream . . .
There will be an end to global warming.
No smoke from factories,
Cars will be eco-friendly,
Ice will stop melting.

I have a dream . . .
Extinction of animals will stop.
Polar bears, tigers, the lot.

But it's just a dream.

Ashley Benton (12)
King Alfred's School

I Have A Dream . . .

I have a dream,
A nightmare,
That one day our Earth
Will not be there,
We will spoil it for ourselves.
The ice caps will melt,
So if we don't take action,
Very soon,
We may be doomed.

I have a dream,
We will sort it out
And so there will be no reason to doubt.
Then the Earth will live to see
Another million years, at least!

Emily Petheram (12)
King Alfred's School

I Have A Dream

I have a dream of no world hunger and that there will be no more wars.
I have a dream that racism will stop and all fights will stop.
I have a dream that there will be no more arguments and all will be happy.

Jordan Eldridge (12)
King Alfred's School

I Dream

I dream about a dream
A dream that's coming true
If you dream about a dream
That dream will come true too
My dream is to be a dancer
A leaper and a prancer
A jumper and a twirler
I dream about a dream
A dream that's coming true.

Lauren Emery (11)
King Alfred's School

Abroad

I have a dream to go abroad
It's a dream, one of my sisters has been
And said it was amazing.
When I see an aeroplane I think of going abroad.

Daryl Roper (12)
King Alfred's School

I Have A Dream!

I have a dream that racism will no longer be,
That we will be all equal.
That we will no longer pollute the Earth.
It's like watching someone you love die.
That black and white will hold hands,
And nobody will think anything of it.
That everyone will be nice to the animals,
And will be in harmony.
That the world will be a free world,
And everyone can roam around wherever they like.
That we keep all of these trees and plants,
Not build them into houses.
That we use water or more safer things,
To fuel our cars without global warming.
That we build more environmentally-friendly things,
To help us with our lives.
And that we have peace in the world.

Ellen Tiso (12)
King Alfred's School

I Have A Dream

When I grow up I could be a leader like Obama,
Having to fear for my life during every step I take.

I could be like Martin Luther King, and get assassinated
For standing up for people who haven't a leg to stand on.

I could be like my beloved father and keep quiet, with my
Family as the limits to my world.

I could aim to be a forensic scientist, slowly bringing light
To the black world of crime . . .

Or, I could grit my teeth, smile, and try to bring a little bit of sunshine into the
Lives of the people around me;
Because you can't shake hands with your enemies
If you have a clenched fist.

Bethan Marshall (12)
King Alfred's School

Imagine

Peace on Earth,
No sound but birds,
No guns being fired,
A white Christmas,
Eating dinner as a family,
All being together at the table,
Everyone being grateful,
Everyone celebrating difference,
Diseases stop spreading,
More lives being saved,
Children's faces once helped,
That everyone can be trusted,
No lies being told,
No more disabilities,
Not having to pretend to smile,
Being happy all the time,
Your wishes coming true,
Hospitals not being needed,
Not having to work,
No earthquakes,
No crime,
No hunger,
Everyone obeying the law,
Having 10 pairs of hands,
Everyone being friends,
The whole world being a family
Everything you can imagine.

Charlotte Johnson (12)
King Alfred's School

I Have A Dream

I have a dream, my dream is that I'm racing
Something that inspires me, is my dad who races
When I look at Thruxton, I want to race
In the future I want to be a British touring car racer.

When I dream, I dream of winning the race
In my dream, I take over people in the race
Then in my dream I dream that I'm the best out of the racers
In the future I will race.

Sam Street (13)
King Alfred's School

Dreams

I once had a dream in my life
But now it's gone far away for good
I need to forget about the past and
Move on to something good.
My life has been amazing from now
New adventures, exposing hot, hot beaches with a tan.
Lanzarote in the sun, music is my life
And hopefully I'll have my real dream.

Alana Savage (13)
King Alfred's School

My Dream Poem

Someone that inspires me is my dad
Because I look up to him,
He's a hard worker and supports his family
He doesn't want to go to work
But he takes the challenge with a half smile.
He is skilful at gaming on the PlayStation 3
And that's why my dad's an inspiration.

Kieran Skuse (14)
King Alfred's School

I Have A Dream . . .

I have a dream . . .
That people are treated with respect,
And nobody is second best.
I have a dream . . .
Nobody has fear
And all around are smiles of cheer.
I have a dream . . .
War is a thing of the past
We so want our world to last
I have a dream . . .
We are all recycling waste
And there is lots of fresh fruit and veg to taste
I have a dream . . .
That people think why jump in the car,
When you don't have to go very far.
I have a dream . . .
That there is fresh air to breathe,
Or there is a lot to achieve.
I have a dream . . .
Now all I need is you,
To help make my dreams come true.

Poppy Broom (12)
King Alfred's School

I Have A Dream

The things I dream about,
The things that you think about,
The world is changing,
The bad things have happened,
But still are happening.

The time is changing,
You and I are changing,
But we're still the same.

The peace is all around us,
People just don't think right when in the war,
The sky is changing,
But they don't know that.

The different views,
The different types.

Remember,
That peace is in the world,
I know that,
But do you?
Think how other people are feeling,
People in the world,
The war,
They must know about peace.

So just think, we're lucky,
But others aren't!

I have a dream
To stop wars
And think about
Peace on Earth!

Stephanie Jeffries (12)
King Alfred's School

Is The Pen Mightier Than The Sword?

'The pen is mightier than the sword,' they say,
We will challenge this today.

The pen and sword have come to fight,
They will battle with all their might.

The sword is sharp and long and smooth,
The pen has only words to use.

The pen and the sword stand face to face,
Sword thinks he will gain first place.

The judge declares, 'Three, two, one, go!'
All Pen's pals shout, 'Oh no!'

Sword says, 'This will be a laugh!
I'll just chop you clean in half!'

Sword swings past, making Pen flinch,
He has missed him by an inch.

Pen isn't feeling very brave,
Then he has a brainwave!

While sword is flying and swinging around,
Pen is scribbling on the ground.

Sword is going to kill without care,
When Pen exclaims, 'Look down there!'

The sword looks down, upon the ground,
And sees some words, so profound.

That he is moved to his very core,
Says, I will fight no more!'

Judge says, 'Well done, Pen, you've won!'
This brings cheers from everyone.

Hooray!

So little children, stop your fighting,
Pick up your pen and start that writing!

Lester Loat (11)
King Alfred's School

I Have A Dream . . .

I have a dream . . .
That there will never be another violent death,
So everyone can take on more breath,
Although it has to be,
It wouldn't if God were me.

I have a dream . . .
That there will never be another lie,
However hard people try,
Although it has to be,
It wouldn't if God were me.

I have a dream . . .
That everybody can be satisfied and fed,
With the people's wine and bread,
Although it has to be,
It wouldn't if God were me!

Tim Bennett (13)
King Alfred's School

Love

Once I had a vision, just a small vision,
But what an amazing vision at that.
It was a calm beauty,
A world without duty,
The duty of worry, poverty and pain,
A life that no one should contain.
Everyone would deserve a chance,
The freedom to leap, jump and prance,
To the open green haloed trees,
Breathing in the freshly squeezed breeze.
Poor innocent children that could be just like you,
Instead have a life making every one of your single shoes.
It is as simple as the purest white dove,
All the world needs is love, love, love.

Jasmine Bussey (12)
King Alfred's School

I Have A Dream

There is a world
A reality world
With smoky air
And melting ice.

There is a world
A dream world
Where I wish to be.

With no pollution
And clean air
With a blink of an eye
And I am there.

There is a world
A reality world
With smoky air
And melting ice.

I have a dream
A wonderful dream
Where there's a world
With no pollution.

But I am afraid
That's only a dream
But it's a dream
That I can see.

Amy Brooks (13)
King Alfred's School

I Have A Dream

I have a dream,
For all the poor to be rich,
Where everyone could share.
No fights with punches, knives and kicks.
All the guns disappear and are never seen again.

I would thank God for that.
But that's not it,
All the drugs need to go,
With the rest of that stuff.
All gone away and never come back.

No drugs, no wars, no none of that,
No cigarettes, abuse or rape, in fact,
No kidnapping, murdering or anything like that,
I want a perfect world.
The innocent left alone and the guilty made innocent.
Where everyone can be friends forever and ever.
That's my dream!

Dec Barron (13)
King Alfred's School

I Have A Dream

I have a dream to make the world a better place,
By being kind to others.

For every right that I can do,
I'm sure to do another.
Every bird that learns to fly,
Another will most probably die.
Because the world is being polluted my friend,
So pick up your litter and let's make amends.

Jessica Brown (13)
King Alfred's School

I Have A Dream

Space inspires me.
It's big and undiscovered
Too big for us to control
But one day I believe we
May be able to hold it all.

Dan Perrin (14)
King Alfred's School

My Dream

I have a dream that I will become successful
Then I will get respect from everyone
I hope that in the future I will own a big company
And become famous.

I have a dream that I will get respect in the future
Like all of the world leaders.
When I become an adult everyone will respect me.

Ishmam Tarafdar (14)
King Alfred's School

My Wishes

I wish I could see my friends from Poland again.
See their happy faces
But that's just my wish.
Maybe my best friends will come to England?
But that's just my dream.
I wish I could be a really good dancer, dance in video clips.
I would like to play a guitar and be a rock star.
But my favourite wish is that people don't die
Because I hate looking at my family and seeing they have sad faces.

Olivia Jankowska (12)
King Alfred's School

Imagine

I wish terrorists were puppets so I could control them,
I would make them listen to others and say sorry.

I wish I was the first person to win the cames
From Berrow.

I wish my parents were back together
So we all would be a lot happier
And that Mum and Dad would get along.

Alex Josham (13)
King Alfred's School

Imagine

I wish
Everyone recycled
Imagine if no one had a dustbin
I wish
There was no way of polluting
So there would be no global warming
I wish
The ice caps weren't melting
So the animals won't die
And the sea wouldn't rise.
I wish
There were no dustbins
So there would be no rubbish to pollute the Earth
I wish
The Earth was a safe place
So no one would get robbed while they're out.
I wish
There were no car crashes
So no one would get hurt.
I wish
No one would get ill
I wish
People would use buses more
So it would not cause as much pollution as all of the cars
I wish
That everyone helped everyone
So jobs would be done quicker
I wish.

Harry Petheram (12)
King Alfred's School

Dream

Dream
When I look at my rescue dog I think of all the animals
that are suffering,
Dream
When he barks I think of all the animals like my pet
that should have been saved,
Dream
When we got him he was scared and his tail was down,
he had dull, sad eyes,
Dream
But now he is a lively happy dog,
his tail is always wagging in the air,
he has bright, shiny eyes and is always ready for a walk,
Dream
When he sat beside the door waiting for Mum to come home,
Dream
His dream came true,
Dream
I think of all the animals waiting to be rescued,
Dream
I have a dream to be a vet, my dream may come true too.

Alice Sands (11)
King Alfred's School

Imagine

When I look at my horse,
And my horse looks back,
He realises how lucky he is to have
A warm comfy bed and lots of hay
And a field to gallop in and *neigh, neigh, neigh.*

Imagine a world where every horse is loved,
With a home to live in and lots of hugs,
Instead of some starving, longing for hay,
No one to love, nowhere to play.

Every day another horse dies,
From being mistreated and lots of lies.
Cruelty to horses just isn't fair,
It's sad and mean and hard to bear.

Imagine a world where every horse is loved,
Where their friends are around them and their life is good,
Instead of some being alone day after day,
No one to love, nowhere to play.

Rachel Butler (12)
King Alfred's School

I Have A Dream

I have a dream of being a drummer.
I have a dream of being a plumber.
I have a dream of being a fryer.
I have a dream of being a DIYer.
I have a dream of being a dog.
I have a dream of being a frog.
I have a dream of being a house.
I have a dream of being a mouse.
I have a dream of being a sunbeam.
I have a dream of being a scream.
I have a dream of being a gran.
I have a dream of being a fan.
I have a dream of being a car.
I have a dream of being a bar.

Roy Jones (12)
King Alfred's School

I Have A Dream

I have a dream that one day I'll fly,
I have a dream that people will listen,
I have a dream that people will not die,
I have a dream.

I am inspired by my parents and sister,
I am inspired by my friends and school,
I am inspired by the people in books and history,
I am inspired.

When I look at the environment it makes me feel sad.
When I look at the wars it makes me feel angry.
When I look at my friends it makes me feel happy.
When I look.

In the future I want money and more.
In the future I want to live forever.
In the future I want to be who I am.
In the future.

I have a dream.

Holly Easterbrook & Stephanie Gray (13)
King Alfred's School

I Have A Dream

I have a dream that nature will flourish and flowers and buds will burst
Like the most beautiful things on Earth.
I have a dream that Mother Nature's hand is
Reaching out on the Earth,
Creating the most beautiful colours.
I have a dream that mammals, birds and insects,
Will form - be born.
I have a dream of children playing in perfect harmony
But then there's me.
I want a dream where I have a friend
To share these dreams with me.

Elizabeth Cahalan (12)
Minehead Middle School

True Friends

True friends inspire in all kinds of ways.
With loyalty, laughter and when we play.
Through friends, we learn something new
And true friends bring much to you.
Life has its ups and downs,
But true friends help turn sad times around.
Although we sometimes disagree,
True friends are there for eternity.

Joel McGuinness (11)
Minehead Middle School

I Have A Dream

If I could I would save the poor
And hope they won't cry anymore
I always hope
That I can cope
For people who are sick
From people who always take the Mick
To stop all the wars
And treat all the sores
For all the pain
Poor people in the rain
If I could see
Someday I could be.

Hannah Newhurst
Minehead Middle School

I Have A Dream

Life happens even when you are asleep
What happens while you are busy planning your life?
Does it happen when you die?
Will it happen when you are alive?

It's possible to do anything.
Black or white, who cares what colour you are?
What person is inside of you?
Don't stop trying, keep trying!

Kirstie Motton (13)
Minehead Middle School

I Would Like . . .

I would like to bring an end to tears and blow away all our fears.
I would like to stop child abuse and put our care into use.
I would like to bring peace and unity and be all that we can be.
I would like to change our minds and make a change to all mankind.

Megan Howe (13)
Minehead Middle School

Change The World

I have a dream
To help global warming
Let's not wait
Until it's too late.

I have a dream
To help world peace
And not fight
From day to night.

I have a dream
To help racism
Black and white
Will together unite.

I have a dream
To help poverty
People won't cry
And starve and die.

I have a dream
To change the world
The world will be peaceful
Happy and joyful.

Jacob Rogers (13)
Minehead Middle School

The World Team

I have a dream
That must be true
To make the world
One big team.

This is all
That I feel
And we still don't know
Who is to rule.

The world has a crack
Divided by colour
Some people in Africa.
Have only a small pack.

I speak to you now
As the world is all raging
It seems that every man and woman
Are having a row!

Today is the day
We all hold hands
And feel God's ray.

Scott Gurnett (13)
Minehead Middle School

Dream Scheme

I have a dream:
To set up a scheme,
That will help poverty in the world now,
And to stop abuse to animals, even a cow.
To stop bullying in school,
And stop wars because they're not cool.
To help orphans on the street,
And the innocent in jail who are hurting their feet.
I will help the sick and poor be rich in heart and soul,
I'll give money and coal,
I want to make Africa a better place,
And stop racism with pace and with haste,
This is what I hope to do
So I don't see people so low too.
I will even give money to a charity
Even all my life savings in clarity.

Ben Dunton (12)
Minehead Middle School

The World, But . . .

The world might not be the best place,
But this should put a smile on your face.
The world is helping without a doubt,
But will not change without our shout.
The world is made from black and white,
But why do we still have to fight.
The world is still at war,
But now we let the blacks through our door.
The world might not be here forever,
But we have to act now, because we're clever.
The world will do its best,
But we have to rise to the test.
The world is a great place really,
But we need to join in clearly.
Even though we're there, nearly,
We need to accept dearly.

Gracie-May Legg (12)
Minehead Middle School

I Have A Dream

I have a dream
A dream to stop all wars,
I have a dream
A dream to stop all guns from killing people,
I have a dream
A dream to stop all murders,
I have a dream
A dream to stop all shouting,
I have a dream
A dream to stop the lonely ones feeling pain,
I wish I could
Could stop all the bullying, and that kids won't go to school,
I wish I could
Could stop all knives from holes and blood,
I wish I could
Could stop all the poor from feeling hungry
I wish I could
Could stop all sickness from spreading pain,
I have a dream
A dream to stop everyone getting hurt,
I have a dream
A dream for the world to be a better place.

Charlene Kendall (13)
Minehead Middle School

Now I'm Rich

Now I'm rich
I'll save your life
Now I'm rich
I'll pay your school life
Now I'm rich
I'll help the poor
Now I'm rich
I save your store
Now I'm rich
I'll pay your rent
Now I'm rich in heart and soul
I have the power to do it all.

Amy Williams (11)
Minehead Middle School

If I Could

If I could change the world,
I'd bring joy and peace to everyone,
If I could change the world,
I'd make sure that every child has fun.

If I could change the world,
I'd join together black and white,
If I could change the world,
I'd help to make things fair and right.

If I could change the world,
I'd put an end to all the wars,
If I could change the world,
I'd also make up different laws.

We can change the world,
If we all do our bit,
But we need to work together,
And not give up or quit.

That's my dream.

Melissa Wells (13)
Minehead Middle School

I Have A Dream

If I could,
I would change this Earth
To be a wonderful place
Where the poor and the rich
The black and the white
The young and the old
Would all come together to be one happy family.

If I could
I would change how people think
So that everyone would think happy thoughts.
From their stubborn minds
And their arrogant voices
To a thoughtful heart
May people see the damage they can do.

So I will change this Earth
We all will,
Make this world safe for everyone and everything
For the animals that are becoming extinct
And the people who have nothing.
Everyone has a heart
So help and do your part.

Sian Hawker (13)
Minehead Middle School

The Homeless

Homeless they are,
And all you do is drive away in your car,
They are hopeful to see you
And what do you do?

You can stand by and think
But just a wink,
Can make them warm inside
You don't need to hide.

To see one of them smile,
Will make your time worthwhile
Love can be amazing
Just feel deep within
Wash out your sins,
Put them in the bin.

Natasha Lothian (12)
Minehead Middle School

Convicts

Why do people kill each other?
In my opinion, I wouldn't bother.
We need to stop this ASAP.
Look on the news and then you'll see.
Nothing wrong with being a nerd.
No more fighting, spread the word.
Life was meant for having fun.
Now those people can't see the sun,
Why'd ya assault him with a broom
Now you're stuck in a tiny room.

Charlie Munson-Hayes (12)
Minehead Middle School

I Have A Dream

When I dream, I dream of you
When I sing, I sing of you
When I love, I love you!

I had a dream last night
It was of me and you on the beach,
Enveloped by the crashing waves of emotion!

Elliott Jaques (13)
Minehead Middle School

I Have A Dream

You may make me a dreamer.
But the dream may never come true.
All it takes is the mind in a right state.
A debt to others.
I'm talking about respect.

Christopher Wilmoth (12)
Minehead Middle School

I Have A Dream!

I have a dream
To make black and white
Friendship reach another height
I have a dream
To help the poor
So they can live their life even more
I have a dream
To prevent war
Stop the injuries and deaths for evermore
I have a dream
For people to treat everyone
Like their son
I have a dream
For the disabled
To be treated like the able
I have a dream
And I hope you will join my team.

William Daughtrcy (13)
Minehead Middle School

As Big As The World

When I'm small I think big,
When I'm big I think bigger,
When I'm alone I'm with God,
When I'm sad I've got friends,
When I'm a child I can help,
When I'm an adult I can help the world,
When I'm tired, I'm awake,
When I'm crying I've got a family,
When I'm part of a team,
I'm as big as the *world!*

William Hole (12)
Minehead Middle School

Save Your Rights

Save a life,
Save the world,
Fight for your rights
It's possible.

One voice,
One person,
Pay it on,
It's possible.

Words change personality,
Imagining words that change the world,
Never, never, never give up!
It's possible.

Imagine having a dream,
Imagine one voice in a crowd
Imagine it's you!

Save a life,
Save the world,
Fight for your rights,
It's possible.

Danielle Holmes (13)
Minehead Middle School

I Have A Dream

The deep dreams I get at night
Always let me see a nice sight,
The sights I see, the sights I get,
Always make me not forget,
That this dream is true,
By involving you,
Whenever I see you in my dreams
I always know this dream is real.

Zoe Williams (13)
Minehead Middle School

Nature

Fresh air
Fluffy white clouds
Shades of green from the rainforests
As if I painted a picture from a storybook
Walking as I go
You don't want to miss even one minute of
Nature.

Amelia Hockin (12)
Minehead Middle School

The Dreamer's Sonnet

'I have a dream,' said Martin Luther King,
Love is a circle with no middle or end
A great big circle, a bit like a ring,
Whether big or small, it is just a bend
We must stop this fighting, it isn't right
Guns, tanks and war just isn't humane
You know we really don't have to fight
It causes so much heartbreak and pain
We're not bloodthirsty creatures, born to kill
Don't let our eyes hate people and turn red
Our lives and destinies we have to fill
And just think what my pal, John Lennon, said,
'You may say I'm a dreamer, but I'm not the only one,
I hope someday you'll join us, and the world will be as one.'

Jake Thompsett (12)
Minehead Middle School

I Have A Dream

I have a dream to inspire the world and influence the future
You are the one voice in the crowd that no one else can hear
You're the one who can change the world
You're the light in the dark, making the difference.
If I could I'd stop the wars and heal the wounded's hurting sores.
If I could I'd mend the parts of Man's lost hope and bleeding hearts.

Ryan Hares (12)
Minehead Middle School

I Have A Dream

In the world today
There are so many things
You can't do or say
What has happened to us?
Have we lost our way?
I wish we could all be kind
And happy each and every day
I dream of this but I fear racism is here to stay
Just maybe one day, it will go away.

Ria Williams (11)
Minehead Middle School

Who Inspires Me Most?

Who inspires me is really hard to think,
There are many people on this Earth,
Some are born within a blink,
Some people are inspired by birth,
But really I think who inspires me best,
Is my mum because she's always there for me,
She helps and supports me, she is also full of zest,
Nature also inspires me, and the honey bee,
Now I have to go, I really have to fly,
This is the end of my poem, goodbye!

Ashley Brooksbank (13)
Minehead Middle School

My Inspiration

My inspiration
Like no other
I give you a snake
It slithers and slides,
And weaves all about
It's cunning, it's agile
Amazing, no doubt
Its tongue, a devil's fork
Its tail, Indiana's whip
His shape shedding skin
Magic to my eye
My inspiration.

Ciaran Barker (13)
Minehead Middle School

The Pain Within

Imagine something, someone,
Who has hurt deep down inside,
It has scarred their life forever,
And the pain will never go away.

Imagine something, someone,
Who now has responsibilities,
They struggle with their life,
But they must let go of the past.

No need to imagine,
There are people like this,
It may not show on their face,
But there is much pain within.

No need to imagine,
This might refer to you,
Just hold your head up high,
And wait to see what the future holds.

Ellie Blandford-Corp (11)
Minehead Middle School

I Have A Dream

My dream is
To see all the world fed
My dream is
To see all wars end
My dream is
The whole world as friends
My dream is
Everyone with enough money to spend
on loads of chocolate cream
My dream is
To look after all of the animals and help people in trouble
My dream is
To make the whole world live happily ever after.
I have a dream.

Shane Archer (11)
Minehead Middle School

I Have A Dream

I have a dream
That there
Will
Never be
War or
Fighting
I have a dream
Where every
Man has a
Right to go to places
And stay alive
I have a dream
That everyone is judged
By his character and
His skin not judged at all
If I could then
I would wish I could
Order people to stop
Being nasty to each other.

Lauren Cornish (12)
Minehead Middle School

If The World Was A Poem

If the world was a poem
The rivers wouldn't stop flowing
The birds would sing
As the church bells ring
What joy that would bring

I have a dream

Killing
War
Misery
Not at all necessary
We need to change this world
We live in
For life and living
To love animals and care
We must not hunt for their hair

To bring peace on Earth

It's our fault the weather is hot
So we should recycle the lot
And maybe if we act fast
The whole world will last
And when we all have hope
Everyone will be happy, even the Pope.

Liam Hosken (12)
Minehead Middle School

You Are!

You are the light in the dark
You are the controller of your own life
You can always follow your heart
You can put a stop to racism
And all the other cruelties in the world
You have a chance to stop it all and not run away
To make it a better place for people to stay
Never, never, never give up.

Katie Roberts (11)
Minehead Middle School

Untitled

Dolphins splashing in the pool
My oh my, that must be cool.
Oh I love the beautiful flowers
They grow so high as tall as towers
Clouds are swinging in the sky
My oh my they are so high.
There is no wind, there is no gale
The dolphins splash with their fins and tail
All the gifts that we bring
Make the dolphins want to sing
The special present is a golden wing
Goodbye dolphins, goodbye spring.

Eva Cameron (11)
Minehead Middle School

My Inspiration

Inspiration, what could inspire me?
An item in a catalogue, paper, or on TV,
A towering bird, a most peaceful tree,
A detailed sketch or a regular person, he or she.

An important person, an idol or friend,
A parent or teacher, someone on whom you can depend.
Even the one who drives you round the bend
Could inspire you to persevere to that bitter end.

Inspirations form, here's an example:
A trophy won, sat proudly on the living room mantle,
The dancing flame on a burning candle
Here's another; the fresh shine of a polished brass handle.

But sadly, none of these inspire me,
Not the handle, the candle or even the peaceful tree.
The only thing that would inspire me,
Would be a piece of A4 paper cut from that old tree!

If you could spare a little more time
I'll explain myself but not in rhyme!

A piece of paper could lead a person to greatness if used correctly.
It could have on it the first draft of a poetic masterpiece
The lyrics and tune of a best seller song,
The plans for an architectural titan or a piece of art
That will be around for many years to come
And will be worth millions for its excellence.
Don't underestimate paper and make the most of it
While it's still here!

Thomas Strachan (13)
Minehead Middle School

180

President Obama

I think he's honest
I think he's kind
I think he knows about hard times

I like the way he talks to us
I like the things he says
I like to think he will be the best President yet

He believes in a better world
He believes in happy families
I believe he will help us create a world of peace and harmony.

Joe Jackson-Clarke (12)
Minehead Middle School

I Have A Dream

This poem is for all of you,
Because you've made it through,
Because of all the shame and pain you felt.
And all of the hurt and bruises he dealt.
You hid it so well,
So that no one could tell,
Because if you were to admit,
You'd be the first to get hit.
This poem is for every time,
He committed that terrible crime.
For when he was meant to read you a story before bed,
But he just hit you and yelled instead.
When the man that was meant to be your dad,
Just hurt you and made you sad.
For the nights he came home drunk and without a care.
He would batter you, but cry, you wouldn't dare.
You were just too ashamed to admit,
That most nights he would break into a fit.
It made you feel so sick,
The times he would silence you with a kick.
When all the other girls and boys,
Had a mum, lots of love and toys
Even the time he shattered your arm,
You didn't get help or raise the alarm.
This poem is especially for you,
And it is the least I can do.
Because now you can hold your head high,
And please don't feel the need to cry.
You proved him wrong, you're still here today,
When you escaped and stopped believing what he would say.
You have a house, a husband and a kid,
You will never treat her the way he did.

Orla Walsh (13)
Minehead Middle School

Inspiration - Haikus

They may be famous
Someone who looks after you,
Or someone special.

You may not know them,
You might be the best of friends,
They are important.

Whoever they are,
Always they inspire you,
To do what you do.

Joshua Chilcott (13)
Minehead Middle School

I Have A Dream

They act like nothing's wrong,
They just get on with things,
They always act so strong,
But all the time I know.

They never hang their heads,
Their lives are just the same.
They could soon be dead,
But all the time I know.

They ignore what people say,
They live a normal life,
They dance around all day
But all the time I know
I know they have cancer.

Phoebe Baker (11)
Minehead Middle School

Who Inspires Me?

I'm inspired by my dad
Because he is completely mad.

He's always happy, never sad
And his jokes are very bad.

I come home from school, he's always hiding
Nowhere original, I always find him.

My dad taught me how to swim
I'd swim like a brick if it wasn't for him.

Every night when I went to bed
I chose a book and the story's read.

If I awoke, with a terrible fright
My dad would comfort me in the middle of the night.

If it wasn't for my dad
I would be like my mum.

Sammy Conway (11)
Minehead Middle School

Autism

Treat us right
A ll of us are still only people like you
Treat us right
U s all united can stop nastiness to people with autism and other problems
Treat us right
T reat us equally, we're people too
Treat us right
I can't do it alone, but together we can
Treat us right
S ee that we are the same
Treat us right
M any people are taken the Mick out of because of their problems
Treat us right!

Simeon Marriott (14)
Ravenswood Special School

Once Upon A Dream

Below the moon, beneath the stars,
I rest my head and close my eyes.
Soon to find the world I love,
A world in which the sun will rise
Upon the meadows of red and white,
Where candy canes glisten in the sunlight,
And the trees that sway in the innocent breeze
Are proudly dressed in silver leaves.
Elephants graze on the mountains above,
Ten thousand humming birds scatter sprinkles of love.
A place where anger is taboo,
And happiness rains over you.
Amongst my cluttered, stressful life,
Which can be full of pain, trouble and strife,
There's always a place full of strawberries and cream,
And that's where I take refuge; once upon a dream.

Laura Garner (15)
West Somerset Community College

The Flower

I have a dream
That a flower sprouts from the seeds of progress,
A delicate bloom that shines and glimmers
In the bleakness of my dream.
The blue and green petals flitter on a cool breeze,
And as I look closely,
I can see that the flower is a haven of serenity.
Within it runs laughter and tranquil smiles
I smile,
I frown -
A new plant is shooting up from the ground.
Born from the seeds of ignorance.
Spikes line the thick stem,
And the plant seems to throb with hatred.
Looking closer, I see that, within the plant,
Courses a flow of bitter tears and innocent blood.
Recoiling in horror, I am paralysed, powerless.
I watch as the vine slowly wraps around the flower
And starts to squeeze . . .
Squeeze the life out of it.
The flower droops and withers,
Crumbling into dust before my eyes.
The vine draws back, satisfied,
And begins a search for another victim.
Waking up suddenly,
I turn on the TV, and see it again -
A vine killing a flower.
A war raging across the globe.
My dream?
My nightmare.

Alex Christmas (14)
West Somerset Community College

188

The Dream

I lay asleep at night,
My body at rest,
My mind alight.

Images in front of my eyes,
My imagination is free,
Until the sunrise.

My mind carries on ticking,
My body awakes,
All works together and gets moving.

Megan Peeks (13)
West Somerset Community College

The Final Game

I have a dream
The cool wind flowing across the grass
The radiant summer's sun beaming across the pitch
The fielders swarming the vast field
I am facing the ball of a bowler
My heart is racing.
My knees are shaking.
The bowler's anger is unleashed with the release of the ball
The gleaming red orb flying towards me with its only intention to
destroy me.

My bat is raised
With all my strength I swing to hit the furiously fast ball
Smash!
The ball is sent flying
Over the heads of astounded fielders.
Crash!
Goes the window of the old lady down the lane
Her angered screams pierce the serene landscape
But even her crow cries are drowned by overwhelming roars of an
elated crowd.

The game is won
I am its hero.

Daniel Cross (15)
West Somerset Community College

I Have A Dream

I have a dream that one day the world will be rid of poverty.
People will not be judged by their colour or creed.
But their personality and size of their heart.
No longer will animals be hunted to extinction.
So women can merely strut the streets in fur coats.

I have a dream that one day everyone will eat, drink and laugh,
No longer will people starve and cry for their lost ones who die from
diseases easily cured.

Wars will be a thing of the past,
People will care for each other,
Help each other,
And not simply judge by what they see.

But then I wake up and look around me,
I see that Man destroys wherever he goes,
He pollutes the planet,
He wages war.
He hunts and kills.

I had a dream of peace but when I woke and I looked around me
I saw the truth of the world.
I heard the gentle sound of bird song
I smelt the sweet scent of a flower which gently sways
In the breeze.
I saw the beauty of nature.
And then I saw people.

Technology has come on,
But has mankind?
How primitive we all still are but how fantastic the natural world is.
Beauty is all around us but we just have to look to find it.
Will there ever be worldwide peace or was it all just a dream?

Jasmine Pyman (14)
West Somerset Community College

Young Writers Information

We hope you have enjoyed reading this book - and that you will continue to enjoy it in the coming years.

If you like reading and writing poetry drop us a line, or give us a call, and we'll send you a free information pack.

Alternatively if you would like to order further copies of this book or any of our other titles, then please give us a call or log onto our website at www.youngwriters.co.uk

Young Writers Information
Remus House
Coltsfoot Drive
Peterborough
PE2 9JX
(01733) 890066